PRAISE FOR *BLACK SHEEP*

"If you have the desire to dictate your own life story, then this practical and powerful read will certainly help you to achieve it."

Phil M. Jones, best-selling author of *Exactly What to Say*

"Brant Menswar's *Black Sheep* takes us on a journey to identify our non-negotiables, speak them into existence and stop winging it when it comes to our life's purpose. Through situational examples, crystal-clear messaging and personal stories—both hilarious and heartbreaking—Brant lays out how YOU can live your black sheep values."

Jim Knight, best-selling author of *Culture That Rocks*

"I've never had a way to actually visualize my core values... until now. I'll be feeding my black sheep on a daily basis from this point forward."

Alison Levine, best-selling author, speaker and American explorer

"*Black Sheep* should come with a soundtrack, because I was bopping my head up and down in agreement as I read each page."

Scott Stratten, six-time best-selling author and black sheep

"This is not, I repeat, *not* your typical 'let's figure out your values' book! What Brant Menswar has put together is verging on genius."
Melissa Wiggins, cofounder of Cannonball Kids' cancer Foundation

"I love being a black sheep. To find the extraordinary, you have to go to the edge. Brant Menswar is the perfect guide for you on this journey. Trust him. Read this book. Reap extraordinary results."
Mitch Joel, author of *Six Pixels of Separation*

"Brant Menswar is a world-class expert at helping people clarify their core values and live their ultimate purpose."
Alan Stein Jr., author of *Raise Your Game*

"We all want to feel that we are living with deliberate intention, which makes *Black Sheep* a great read for those seeking their purpose and looking for help in finding it."
Kay Rawlins, cofounder of Orlando City Soccer Club (MLS Franchise)

"In this illuminating and compelling book, Brant Menswar delivers mic-dropping wisdom that will set you on a path to living with intention and purpose. *Black Sheep* takes you on a journey of defining your *what*, so you can live your *why*."
Phillip Stutts, best-selling author of *Fire Them Now*

BLACK

BRANT MENSWAR

SHEEP

Unleash the Extraordinary, Awe-Inspiring, Undiscovered You

PAGE TWO
BOOKS

Cataloguing in publication information is available from Library and Archives Canada.
ISBN 978-1-989603-44-4 (hardcover)
ISBN 978-1-989603-58-1 (ebook)

Page Two
www.pagetwo.com

Cover and interior design by Peter Cocking
Cover and interior illustrations by Theo Menswar
Printed and bound in Canada by Friesens
Distributed in Canada by Raincoast Books
Distributed in the U.S. and internationally by
Publishers Group West, a division of Ingram

20 21 22 23 24   5 4 3 2 1

www.findyourblacksheep.com

To those longing for a
push to pursue something more.
This is it.

Contents

Introduction

WHAT MATTERS MOST TO YOU

GOAL #1 ACCOMPLISHED. Write a book so unique, so powerful that a mere glance at the cover compels a reader to look inside. My question is, why did you pick it up? Answering that is like trying to identify a single white sheep among a flock of five hundred others.

I have no idea why you picked up this book, and my guess is you might not know either... yet.

Maybe the image of the black sheep on the cover resonated deep within you. For most of us, the idea of being a black sheep has a negative connotation. The black sheep of the family (or the office) is often understood as an outcast or someone who's difficult to work with. However, the demonizing of black sheep is based on a misunderstanding. And there are many complex reasons why you might feel like black sheep. Maybe you've been so amazing at your profession that you've separated yourself from the flock, but you don't really know what formula propelled you to those heights.

In any case, you're going to have to Tarantino this shit for a moment or two, and go back to move forward. In other words, an understanding of the events and actions that got you to where you are now will provide the answers you seek and a path to move forward.

What I'm about to tell you is so accepting and powerful, it will transform your life, thoughts and beliefs. Have you ever wondered why actual black sheep are cast aside, ostracized and not valued like the rest of the flock? The reason shocked me. *A black sheep's wool cannot be dyed.*

That's right. A black sheep is 100 percent, authentically original. It cannot be influenced, changed or molded into something it isn't by outside forces. Do you understand the implications of that? You may have mixed feelings about identifying as a black sheep. But if your goal is to be who you were uniquely created to be, then you are almost there now.

You possess a power within you that you don't even understand yet. A power that will allow you to manifest incredible things in your life in a practical, tangible way. I'm not talking about some bullshit hocus-pocus manifestation mantra. I'm talking about the ability to activate the most important core values within you— what I call your "black sheep values"—and use them to choose and fulfill your purpose.

START WITH *WHAT*

So many of us have been schooled to start with *why*. So we have traveled down that path and defined our *why*, only to find that nothing has changed in our lives. What happened? You may have done exactly what you thought you were told to do, but you still aren't seeing a transformation in your personal or professional life.

Guess what? If you're like the rest of us, you got your *why* wrong, because for your *why* to be accurate, you have to start with *what*. What are your non-negotiables? What are the core values at the very foundation of who you are, those traits that, no matter what someone says or how someone influences you, cannot be altered, dyed or changed?

Those core values are *your* black sheep.

Finding your black sheep values—the one-of-a-kind combination that makes you distinct from everyone else on the planet—enables you to live your truth, to be your 100 percent authentic, extraordinary self. There is a palpable power in owning your truth. More than likely, you've experienced that power in someone a few times in your life. It can feel like you're in the presence of a human magnet. You find yourself attracted to that power in an almost otherworldly way. It's both comforting and exhilarating. Inspiration surges through you, the way you might feel after seeing *Rocky* for the first time—ready to take on whatever the world throws at you.

Your black sheep are the deeply held core values that make you an original. They cannot be altered, dyed or changed.

When you discover your black sheep, you create an even more powerful opportunity: the chance to choose when and where your core values appear. To track their flocks, farmers place one black sheep for every hundred white sheep. Every morning a sheep farmer wakes up and looks out at all the sheep in the field. If they have five hundred sheep in their care, they should see five black sheep. If they don't see those five, they know something is wrong. Despite not being valued like the white sheep, the black sheep are what the farmer looks to first. Like you, their uniqueness allows them to stand out.

YOUR PERCEPTION IS POWERFUL

Legendary illusionist Harry Houdini famously said, "What the eyes see and the ears hear, the mind believes." This sentiment begins to explain why I want you to place your black sheep front and center in your life. Your view of the world is filtered through what you believe. When you strategically choose the times and places your black sheep appear, you help craft the narrative that other people are constantly creating about you, and you maximize your impact on them.

This is why you have to start with *what*. Your *what* is your core values, which dictate your *why* (your purpose), which governs your *how* (your mission, or the actions you take to live out that purpose). It looks like this:

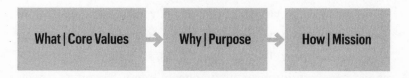

| What | Core Values | Why | Purpose | How | Mission |

You have to discover your *what* and then choose your *why*. Those rarely change. They are like the roots of a tree. Your *how* is like the branches that grow in all directions. Your *how* always changes. Every new opportunity—in fact, every item on your daily agenda— is a chance to fulfill your mission through the way you act.

We often think of a mission as a calling or vocation. But a mission is simply an important assigned or self-imposed task. Think of your daily tasks as missions. With every new conversation comes a new opportunity to fulfill your mission and live out your purpose.

If you've felt uninspired or that living out your mission is like trying to catch a bag of squirrels, you aren't alone. When you don't start with *what* (your core values) and use that to inform your *why* (your purpose), your *how* can be messy and confusing. Even accomplishing a big goal can feel like a soulless win. That happens when your mission is not aligned with your purpose. Your purpose is the reason you exist on this planet. But, as important as it is to define your purpose for yourself, only a tiny fraction of the population actually does so.

Could you tell me in a few succinct sentences what your life's purpose is, why you chose it and how you engage with it every day?

It's okay. Neither can 99 percent of us. Some believe that's because our purpose changes over the course of our lives. As we get older and wiser, the reasons we do things shift. But that's simply not true. That's people confusing their purpose—which doesn't change—with their missions, which change constantly.

How many recent retirees do you know who are busier now than when they were working full time? They try a million different ways to fulfill a purpose they never defined. An aimless *how* can keep you busier than a mosquito at a nudist colony. To understand your purpose, you need to ask some tough questions, accept some difficult answers, search for proof and build up the courage to use what you've learned. Because it seems like a daunting journey, most people never take the first step.

What a missed opportunity!

Those who are willing to search for, find and tend to their black sheep values control the narrative of their lives. They refuse to rely on luck or accidents to find success. They make deliberate decisions about where and when their black sheep appear, and they put those values into action to fulfill the purpose they have chosen.

Does that describe you?

It didn't always describe me. A catastrophic event in my life forced me to discover my black sheep. It took cancer... in my oldest son. It took being faced with an impossible decision, making the wrong decision and living with the repercussions of it. It doesn't have to be that way for you. I want to help you build such a strong foundation in your life that nothing can tear it down. No matter the size or strength of the storm you are facing.

It is my hope that you take some time to use this book as a guide or workbook to find the crucial answers you need to live your best life. There are resources in these pages to help you on your quest. If you are willing to do the work, by the time you are done with this book, you will be able to do the following:

Find your black sheep (those core values that will guide your life).

Choose your purpose (by activating your core values, so that you live with deliberate intention).

Program your values to appear on demand (being deliberate about when, where and how your black sheep show up in your daily life for maximum impact).

Live as the awe-inspiring person you were always meant to be.

Maybe you're crushing life right now and want to continue honoring the commitments you need for sustainable success. Or maybe you're feeling lost, uninspired and completely confused about what direction to go in and who you want to be. Wherever you're at, this book will guide you through the process of finding answers, embracing truths and empowering yourself to let your black sheep run proud and free.

If you are anything like me, you want to experience some quick wins and then decide whether it's worth investing more of your time to continue reading. I've got you. My promise to you is no fluff (although a peanut butter sandwich is only living up to half its potential without fluff). We will focus on the things that are crucial to see results. Anything less than transformational is a failure. Those are the stakes... take them or leave them.

To do anything "on purpose," you have to know what your purpose is. That requires you to define your core values—to find your black sheep. Most people don't do that because accountability sucks; it flies in the face of the radical freedom we all love. But if you haven't found and activated your black sheep, it's impossible to do anything on purpose. If you don't know your core values, inevitably you are an unconscious creator of your own reality. Until you define your black sheep, you are winging it.

1

UNCONSCIOUS CREATORS

It's time to wake up.

FROM THE mid-1800s till the turn of the century, the United States experienced an explosive growth in population. As the country basked in opportunity, Americans found themselves with a little extra time and money, and they were looking for ways to spend them both. To meet that growing demand, and as the interest in American theater boomed, thousands of playhouses were built.

During this time, actors had a hard time keeping up with the variety of plays on offer and they often quickly had to fill in for fellow entertainers who were sick or unable to perform their roles. Because of the last-minute nature of the problem, actors would have to learn their lines offstage while a play was being performed. This practice of frantically learning their parts in the wings of the theater became known as "winging it."

Fast-forward 125 years and, shockingly, we are a country that has adopted this practice, not as a means to deal with emergencies, but as a way of life. We make rapid decisions, not based in the deep-rooted core values that guide our true north, but in the swirling, volatile tornado of our emotions—all the while hoping our choices have favorable outcomes that might help our careers, appease our emotional demons or improve our tenuous relationships.

If you are waking up every morning, going to work, making hundreds of decisions that impact your personal and professional life and you have no idea how to identify your black sheep values—*you are winging it.*

You are navigating life backstage, frantically making decisions in the moment while the performance of a lifetime is quickly slipping away from you.

I know I just pissed some readers off. How dare I question your intentions and the way you live? You may be pulling a bunch of values out of your hat at this very moment and holding them up, yelling, "See? I know what I value!"

But do you? Can you tell me exactly what your non-negotiables are, give multiple examples of acting them out over the course of your life and explain specifically why you concluded that these core values mean the most to you? Can you tell me how you honor them every day, with deliberate intention?

For most of us, the answer to all those questions is no.

And therein lies the source of the problem that has spread across this country, like a cybervirus taking down every computer in its destructive path. Our black sheep are lost.

If your boss came into your office tomorrow, presented you with the company's goals for next year and asked you how you plan on reaching them, what would you say? Would you look your boss in

If you're not living with deliberate intention, you're winging it.

the eye and say, "Well, I guess I'm going to wing it"? Of course not! You'd be out on your ass looking for a new job. You would present your boss with a plan, back it up with data and proudly reveal your timeline for staying on track. That's how people move forward and up in organizations.

When it comes to our personal lives, however, it seems most of us aren't willing to invest the time to plan how to move anything forward. We don't show ourselves the same respect we show our superiors at work. Why?

Because accountability sucks.

That's why we can't lose weight, why we can't stop smoking, why we can't save money... the list goes on and on. Do you know what sucks even more than accountability? That it starts with you. Most of us buck against the idea of being accountable for our own successes and failures.

But the reality is that you are held accountable to things all the time. At work, you have to meet deadlines, budgets, goals... do you think these TPS reports are going to print themselves? You accept this type of accountability because it comes with the job. If you are going to work for a particular company, you have to play by its rules. But what about *your* rules?

Wait, *what*?

What are the rules that come with the job of being you? Your black sheep values set forth the rules that are most important to you. In doing so, they provide a structure that gives you the freedom to say yes to what you want and no to what you don't want, without battling any feelings of guilt. More importantly, they allow you to live with deliberate intention and stop winging it.

To experience any type of transformation, it is crucial to understand the difference between being intentional and acting with deliberate intention.

BE DELIBERATE WITH THAT SHIT

I have spent the better part of the last twenty years in the music business. I lived the dream of being a real-life rock star, signing record deals and traveling the world performing as the front man for Fort Pastor in the Christian music market before forming the popular blues/rock band Big Kettle Drum with my bandmate, JT Keel, in 2009. In the summer of 2017, we traveled to Los Angeles to record our fifth album, *I Thought You'd Be Bigger*, with the incomparable Carla Olson, who has played with The Textones and produced legends. Part of being purists and wanting to capture our original tone meant that JT and I drove from Orlando to L.A. to bring our own equipment to the studio. Over a hot, sticky week we recorded with legendary musicians like Barry Goldberg on organ, Tony Marsico on bass and Don Heffington on drums—an all-star group of guys that made this a once-in-a-lifetime experience for us. Look them up... it's ridiculous who they've played with.

After we wrapped up recording our parts, we began the long journey back across the country, reveling in the aftermath of such incredible musicianship. At about six in the morning, after a night of driving, we crossed the New Mexico state line. The sun was coming up, making it hard to see over the steering wheel. We were the only car on the road for miles... Well, one other car was on the road. A police car.

As the officer walked up to the window, I frantically asked JT why on earth I had been pulled over. I knew I hadn't been speeding. Was a taillight out? Were my tags expired? Did we have a dead body in the trunk?

"You know you were traveling in the left-hand lane, sir?" the officer asked.

Um... okay, I thought. *What's the problem? There isn't another car in sight.*

"It's against the law in this state to travel in the left-hand lane, unless you are passing," he said.

The good news is that I professed my ignorance and he let me off with a warning. And I quickly adopted the right-hand one as our lane of choice for the remainder of the drive home.

Here's the gist of my story: I knew the direction I was heading and my ultimate destination. I was being intentional—but I wasn't acting with *deliberate intention*. Instead, I was zoned out, headed in the right direction but in the wrong lane, unaware of the rules. That describes how many of us choose to live our lives.

A lot of values are important to you, but which ones are you unwilling to compromise on? Those are your non-negotiables.

We disregard our own bottom-line standards, so we don't have any-thing to hold ourselves accountable to. If we knew our own rules, would we deliberately break them? Most of us don't like breaking rules. The first step in following our own rules is to be aware of them and to be conscious creators of our own reality.

As an unconscious creator, you may eventually head in the direction you want to go, but you'll never get there *on purpose*. To reach your destination, you will need to seduce Lady Luck and pray for no diversions. Is that how you want to live? Relying on sheer chance and fortune? Being part of the larger flock of white sheep, ignorantly building someone else's dream? Then simply be intentional, and leave it at that.

But for deliberate intention, you need to find and account for your black sheep. Deliberate intention challenges you to dis-tinguish your non-negotiables from the things that are merely important to you. I guarantee that the list of what's important to you is an exhaustive one and, if you try to make every item on it a regular priority, you will only muddy your actions. When fifty things are important to you, how do you honor all of them consis-tently? You don't. You can't. But you try, and then feel ashamed and inadequate, depressed and anxious, when you see that your perfect intentions fell short.

Are you ready to find out what makes you stand out from the flock? Are you prepared to shift what's within your power to change? I have a friend who likes to needle me over what she calls my "philanthropy days," when I place everyone else's needs above my own. If your calendar is filled with too many of those days, you'll likely be overwhelmed and you won't have the time or energy to devote to the things that will move your life upward. She describes it like this: "With every rung you climb on the ladder, you reach new opportunities. But if you start reaching down to lift others up before your footing is sure, the only thing possible is that they'll pull you back down." I had to learn that sometimes, in order to best serve people, you have to put yourself first. If you can reach your full potential, the impact you can have on those you love and the world around you is exponentially amplified.

"SHEEP THRILLS" REMINDER

What: Become a conscious creator and stop winging it.

Why: If you don't live with deliberate intention, your success will either be by accident or by luck.

How: To find your black sheep, you need to distinguish between your non-negotiables and what's merely important to you.

Good decisions are the key to consistent, long-lasting success. Perhaps the most common misunderstanding about that statement is what constitutes a "good" decision. Most people judge good or bad based on outcomes, but the quality of a decision has nothing to do with its results—because you cannot control outcomes. You can only control the deliberate intention that you put into a decision. If you follow what I call the "decision supply chain," your choices will be good every time, and success will be only a decision away.

2

GOOD DECISIONS

Results have nothing to do with making a good or bad choice.

LOVE EVERYTHING about coffee. It's my beverage of choice. The smell of the beans, the gurgling sound of it brewing, the deep caramel color and that first sip every morning as I try to pick out the subtleties of its heritage. It borders on an obsession.

Over the years, I have learned that for me to have a consistently good cup of coffee, I need to honor three specific rules: (1) I need to know its origin. Where were the beans harvested? I prefer beans from certain areas of the world. (2) I need to know that it was ethically sourced and thoughtfully produced. The coffee industry is notorious for using slave labor to harvest its product. I need my coffee to come from an organization that values investing in some of the poorest parts of the world and that provides a living wage for workers. I also want to know that the coffee roaster cares for those beans like their own children, giving them everything they need to achieve their full potential. (I told you I have a problem.) (3) I need to respect my mood. If I'm upset or angry, even the best cup of coffee will taste bitter and I will pick it apart and call out every fault before I judgingly pour it down the sink. But if I can honor these three criteria, I have the best chance of enjoying a good cup of coffee.

I was discussing this with a friend, who quipped that if I go through *all that* for a good cup of coffee, what must I go through to make a good decision... and the seed was planted. As someone who studies, speaks and writes about human behavior, I started down a rabbit hole of research about what makes decisions good, and how to consistently make them so. To my surprise, my coffee rules are eerily aligned with what my research on choices revealed.

To make a good decision, we must do three things:

Account for our core values (our non-negotiables).
Consider all the facts.
Honor our feelings in the moment.

I call this the "decision supply chain." It's that simple. These are the three basic steps between each of us and a good decision. Take them all, and a good decision is achieved, regardless of the outcome.

Discovering this, I felt as though I had solved one of the world's great problems. I imagined revealing my findings to audiences around the globe during my talks and watching a massive transformation take place while I planned for my Netflix special (move over, Brené) and waited for the call to schedule my long overdue *Time* magazine cover.

In the decision supply chain, you account for your core values, consider all the facts and honor your feelings in the moment.

I truly wasn't prepared for what occurred next. I walked off stage after stage to standing ovations. I received countless messages from audience members who had "life-changing" experiences during my talks, and my speaking schedule exploded. How could it possibly get any better?

And then it happened. *Nothing.*

No transformational change. No earth-shaking action. No tsunami of good decisions leading to a cultural revolution. How could this be? What was stopping the progress? Why weren't people living the life of fulfillment they were so desperate to achieve? I had provided all the necessary ingredients for unprecedented life change. I'd left no stone unturned. I'd given step-by-step instructions. Still, the revolution I expected remained at bay. Why?

As I sat in a quaint little coffee shop in downtown Cocoa Village one morning, enjoying my single-source pourover, I stared out the window at the passersby frantically trying to get their shit together before embarking on another anxiety-ridden day. That's when the answer hit me.

The transformation I dreamed of hadn't happened yet because people hadn't nailed down the first step. They hadn't identified the core values that are crucial to step one of the decision supply chain.

Recall that core values, your black sheep, are your non-negotiables. If you don't have those defined, then what are your decisions based on? *I'll take F-words for $1,000, Alex.*

No, not that word, you filthy sailor. I'm talking about *feelings.*

Feelings serve an important role in the process, but a tug-of-war between your black sheep values and your feelings is at the center of the battle to make good decisions. Even when you've found and empowered your core values, feelings can have the strength of Hercules, the notoriously bad judgment of a crack addict and the stability of North Korea. Allowing your emotions to lead the decision-making process is like asking your drunk uncle to give the blessing at Thanksgiving dinner—dangerous! Feelings change constantly and thus should not be the sole driver of decisions. When you let that happen, you're much more likely to make catastrophically bad decisions.

I understand this pitfall intimately, as I'm still recovering from my life's worst decision.

In 2012 my eldest son, Theo, was diagnosed with a rare blood cancer called myelodysplastic syndrome and he required a bone marrow transplant to survive. After a short search for a suitable match, Theo received his transplant on August 12, 2012, and we began a 263-day nightmare in the Kids Beating Cancer Pediatric Transplant Center at Florida Hospital in Orlando.

While we waited for Theo's body to accept the new marrow, we were warned of something called graft-versus-host disease, or GVHD, which happens when the donated bone marrow doesn't recognize the transplant environment and begins to attack the body. Everyone who receives a bone marrow transplant experiences GVHD in one of its four stages. Most people find themselves

Constantly changing feelings can pull us off balance. Our black sheep help us stand firm.

in stage one or two and recover quickly. If the disease progresses to stage four, it can be fatal. Our overachieving son was apparently shooting for stage nine; his body was so riddled with the disease that it quickly put his life in danger. The only treatment at this point is to go to extreme measures: suppress the immune system and hope for the best. Unfortunately, this treatment places the body at great risk for infection. That's where we found ourselves with Theo.

While his immune system was suppressed, he contracted a deadly fungus called mucormycosis. The proper treatment for this infection is to boost the immune system so the body can attack the fungus. That wasn't an option, so we found ourselves in an impossible situation. The two issues created a zero-sum game. On March 23, 2013, the medical team pulled my wife and me into a room and explained that no matter which issue they treated, the other would take his life. They suggested we say our good-byes to our son, as they thought he wouldn't make it through the night.

My head and heart were swirling like an EF5 tornado and my ability to find shelter was nonexistent. I grabbed my wife's hand as we walked back, sobbing, to Theo's hospital room to tell our younger son, Brady, that we were going to have to say good-bye to his big brother. As I sat on the edge of Theo's bed, I made the worst decision I have ever made. I said good-bye. Hearing your child quietly whisper "I'm going to miss you, Daddy," is something you don't get over. It haunts you.

But meanwhile, something miraculous happened.

My younger brother Todd, who lives 1,500 miles away in New Hampshire, was devastated that night when he received the news. After he said good-bye to Theo, he hung up the phone and did something that would change the course of our lives. He filmed a video of himself holding poster boards explaining Theo's case and pleading for help from anyone who could contribute, and uploaded it to YouTube. Almost overnight, the video had 500,000 views. We started to receive calls from people all over the world who believed they could help. The callers included brilliant doctors with uniquely specific experience in the challenges we were facing.

Come to find out, the zero-sum game our doctors perceived wasn't entirely true. An experimental treatment would allow us to address both diseases at the same time—an option our doctors hadn't been unaware of.

At that point, I hadn't taken the time to find my core values and didn't know how to filter my actions through the things that mattered most to me. I allowed solely my feelings to drive my actions, and I didn't use my black sheep values to temper my emotions, to help me ask the tough questions and explore the whole truth in my family's situation. My feelings blinded me to the possibility that a larger truth existed.

Sometimes the truth in the room is a limited one. I relate it to searching for a house on a real estate app. If you narrow your search to an overly restrictive set of parameters, your results are

Facts can exist beyond any limits you might set for them. Open up your search to find the real truth.

confined. Your perception of what's possible is skewed. But if you expand your search, even by a short distance, the results can grow remarkably. This is why the second part of the decision supply chain is paramount. We need to consider *all* the facts, not just the facts in the room.

Within twenty-four hours of my brother's video going viral, we had a crazy plan to try to save Theo's life. It included a machine that spins blood so fast that it separates the white cells from the red cells and exposes them to ultraviolet light. This would kill the T cells that were causing all the problems and would give Theo a fighting chance.

It worked.

Theo's body began to recover and, after a few more months in the hospital, we were able to bring him home. He recently celebrated his twenty-second birthday and is pursuing a career in graphic design. In fact, he designed the black sheep logo on the cover of this book that also rests on my right forearm, an inked reminder of what's possible when our black sheep are front and center.

We couldn't foresee the fairy-tale outcome of our living night-mare. In the moment the doctors told us to say our good-byes, our feelings suffocated any other possible option. How are you supposed to believe in fairy tales when real life is crashing down all around you? Sometimes your feelings don't leave room for fairy tales.

Those desolate moments breed the worst decisions. My memory of sitting on the edge of Theo's bed and saying good-bye has been the cause of many sleepless nights in the years since. The question gnawing the inside of my head plays over and over in an endless loop: *I wonder if he thinks I gave up on him...*

I made a horrible decision in that moment because I hadn't identified my black sheep. If I had known then what I do now, the conversation with my son would have been completely different. It would have had an enormous, positive influence on his life that is only possible from unrelenting hope (which, you'll learn, is one of my core values).

Hope drove me to write this book. I want you to believe in hope, too. You might be beating yourself up over how shitty your life looks at the moment, using failed outcomes to blame yourself for all the bad decisions you have made. I understand. We all do it. But, as my story is meant to show you, outcomes have nothing to do with whether your decisions are good or bad. So take the gloves off, go back to your corner and catch a breather. As Rocky Balboa said to Clubber Lang in *Rocky III*, "You ain't so bad! You ain't so bad!"

WHAT'S YOUR MEASURE?

How do you know when you've made a good decision? If you are like the thousands of people who I have asked that question to over the last year, your answer will be based on some sort of outcome:

> **"The results are there!"**
> **"People are happy with the decision."**
> **"It felt good!"**
> **"No one got hurt!"**

Every time I pose this question from the stage, I receive similar answers... all of which are wrong. Using an outcome to justify whether a decision is good or bad is something behavioral scientists call "outcome bias." Individuals and organizations alike mistakenly use outcomes to measure the value of decisions. In fact, many organizations promote employees based solely on their outcomes. This is a dangerous and uninformed practice for one simple reason: *You can't control outcomes.*

Unless your name is Gandalf or Glinda, you don't have that kind of power. All you can control is the deliberate intention that goes into your decision-making process. Once the decision is made, it's out of your hands.

My fellow control freaks, as you wipe your sweaty palms and rock back and forth at the mere thought of what you just read, I feel it, too. It's incredibly uncomfortable to realize that outcomes are out of your control.

Tying whether you feel good to an outcome can bite you in the ass.

If you shift your desire from controlling the outcome to finding your black sheep values, uncovering all the facts and honoring your feelings in the moment, you powerfully improve the chances of achieving what you want, without tying your happiness to a result. That is the goal.

With my son, I made a bad decision that wasn't based on my values, and we had the best possible result. Would you promote an employee who constantly makes decisions that are out of alignment with your organizational values, but who somehow keeps achieving good results? It's one of the quickest ways to destroy company culture.

Start looking at *how* you make decisions instead of your outcomes. Approach every situation armed with the power of your black sheep. Definitely lead with them as you start the decision supply chain. By leading with your core values, you also help yourself navigate the potential field of "feelings land mines" that our egos love to run through.

THE TUG-OF-WAR

The last step of the decision supply chain—honoring your feelings in the moment—challenges the level of your commitment to any decision. As I said earlier, feelings play an important role in the process. If you make a decision without acknowledging what you're feeling about your choice at that moment, you make Hulk angry. Hulk no like angry. To stay committed to a decision, you have to look at the tug-of-war between your values and your feelings.

On one hand, if you decide something solely based on your black sheep values and ignore your feelings, your commitment can be swayed by powerful unacknowledged emotions. On the other hand, if you choose a course of action solely based on your feelings and ignore your black sheep, the possibility of violating one of the values you hold most dear will threaten your ability to keep your commitment.

If you don't want your feelings to be the sole driver of your decisions and you don't want to ignore your values, then who should win the tug-of-war? The answer, it might surprise you to learn, is neither.

You need to keep a healthy tension between your values and feelings. Let me explain. Our feelings often like to push us into the future to party with uncertainty and doubt, the troublemakers. We get caught up in the Land of What Ifs and Could Bes and project possible outcomes that fuel our insecurities. Using your values that have been developed over the course of your life to serve as an anchor prevents you from being pulled off balance and helps you stay in the present. If you want to give yourself the best opportunity to make a good decision, you need to be in the present, and a healthy tension between your black sheep and your feelings allows you to do that, as does knowing your motivation.

REWIND TO FAST-FORWARD

Motivation is a scary word. It fills up half of our Instagram feeds with images of sports cars, bikini models, luxury homes, private jets and wine and cheese... heavy on the cheese. Hundreds of books have been written about motivation, and I don't want to minimize the complexity of understanding what drives us. I told you in the introduction that you have to go back before you can move forward. This is another such case.

When we are kids, our motivation is much easier to diagnose because of the raw behavior and lack of understanding that every two-year-old wears like a badge of honor. In the study of what motivates children to make certain decisions, researchers often use the Four Functions of Behavior, a framework that looks something like this:

Sensory: Children are motivated by what feels good. For example, infants like to bite on frozen teething toys because they soothe their sore gums. If the biting gives the sensory input the infants need, they will continue to chew on the toys.

Escape: Children are motivated by avoiding an undesirable situation. For example, a parent says, "Eat your broccoli," and a child runs from the dinner table.

Attention: Children are motivated by social interactions. For example, a child screams bloody murder in the middle of the grocery store. If screaming gets the desired attention, then the screaming will repeat.

Tangible: Children are motivated by wanting access to a specific item or activity. For example, a child pulls the hair of another to get access to a video game. If the child gets the video game, the hair pulling will resurface.

In my experience, these motivating factors still apply to forty-eight-year-olds. Adapted for an adult, the Four Functions of Behavior might look something like this:

Sensory: We are motivated by something that feels good. Clara volunteers at the local soup kitchen because empathy is one of her core values; the feeling she gets when she serves others motivates her to keep going back.

Escape: We are motivated by wanting to avoid an undesirable situation. Rose takes the long way around the office to her desk because Johnny is a douchebag and she doesn't want to have to say no, again, to him asking her out.

Attention: We are motivated by the desire for attention from others. As the office gossip, Janice likes to talk shit around the water cooler because of the attention she receives from her colleagues. As long as people keep feeding the monster, the monster continues to come back for food.

Tangible: We are motivated by getting access to a specific item or activity. The sales manager announces that a $500 bonus will be given out to the person with the highest sales this month. The desire for the extra money motivates each member of the sales team to work harder.

Often when we struggle to decide something, we have competing motivators—more than one thing driving our behavior—and it can upset the tug-of-war balance between our feelings and our values. When we understand the motivation behind our behavior, we give ourselves the best opportunity to stay committed to the decisions we make.

Let's say I have a motorcycle. People don't buy motorcycles because they get great gas mileage or because they are practical. People buy motorcycles because of how riding one makes them feel. This is a *sensory* motivation. So as I take my bike out for a ride each weekend, I enjoy the leaning into the corners and the wind in my hair that provides the sensory input I desire.

It isn't long before my wife decides she wants to come along on the rides. So she jumps on the back and we ride together. While we are cruising, she notices that other wives are wearing these leather vests with cool patches on them. "What are those?" she asks. I explain that you get the patches by being part of a motorcycle club that hangs out together. "I want a cool patch and vest!" she says. This is a *tangible* motivation. She wants access to the swag from the local motorcycle club.

Understanding your motivation for a decision helps you stay committed to it.

Here's the challenge: for that to happen, we have to join the club. I'm not motivated by the social interaction. In fact, I am now motivated by *escape*! I want to avoid hanging out with others. I simply want to ride the bike. My wife and I have competing motivators. What do I do? How do I restore the balance?

I look to my black sheep. Rather than just give in and be upset that I didn't get my way, or ignore the wishes of my wife and have her be upset with me, I can look to my values and keep the healthy tension between my values and my feelings as I examine what matters most to me. One of my black sheep is family. So I need to respect my wife's wishes and find a way to make this work. I check the list of local motorcycle clubs and where they meet to get all the facts about what's possible. I review the potential choices with my wife and suggest we go down to a local motorcycle dealership and join a club so she can get her cool patch and vest. I also suggest that we mingle with other members for about thirty minutes and then invite some to join us on our ride for the day. She gets her swag. I get to ride. Win–win.

When we follow the decision supply chain, making good decisions is easy; the decision supply chain helps us use deliberate intention to move toward our desired goals. But just because we might achieve a goal, doesn't mean we are doing it *on purpose*.

What: A good decision begins with your black sheep values, takes in all the facts and also accounts for how you feel in the moment. This is the decision supply chain.

Why: Outcomes can't be controlled. But how you make decisions can be.

How: Practice staying true to your black sheep values by using the decision supply chain.

We all inherently desire to know our purpose. Even Aristotle documented our longing to find our *why*. Yet only a fraction of us actually do find it. That's because we've been misled our entire lives. You don't find your purpose. You choose it. To make a meaningful choice, you have to discover your non-negotiables—those undyeable black sheep values that live within you and make you an original. With the activation of your five core values, you can choose a purpose and stay committed to what matters most to you.

3

THE BIGGEST LIE ABOUT PURPOSE

Purpose: it's not a mystery, it's a choice.

BELIEVE "ON PURPOSE" is one of the most misused phrases in the English language. We use it to describe something done intentionally, but I'd like to suggest a different definition. To do something on purpose means to act in alignment with your greater purpose (the reason you get up every day), and therein lies the problem. As you have already seen, most of us have no idea what our purpose is.

Purpose is the word of the moment. It's everywhere. Hustle culture tells you to use it to get up at four in the morning and check your vision board. Simon Sinek directs leaders to start with it to inspire action. The latest research confirms there is no better way to build loyalty, unite teams and amplify performance. We have elevated *purpose* to the heights of Everest with about the same odds of obtaining it as reaching the summit of the world's highest peak.

I hate climbing. So let's break it down.

Purpose is the reason for which something exists. The purpose of a hammer is to drive nails. The purpose of a pen is to write. The purpose of a toilet plunger is... you get it. When we talk about the purpose of our being here, things get existential and unclear. We act like the answer is written on an ancient scroll buried deep in a mystical tomb.

Stop it!

Stop placing purpose out of your reach. Stop acting like finding your purpose is a dangerous quest only to be ventured by the bravest of souls. You don't have to be Indiana Jones and you've already found the Temple of Bullshit. When I ask crowds why they haven't found their purpose, I get the same three answers:

"Life gets in the way!" Life is *always* in the way. What you're really saying is that this isn't a priority and, because accountability sucks, you would prefer to wing it.

"It changes!" No, it doesn't. Have you ever tried to use a hammer as a screwdriver? Our *what* (our core values) and our *why* (our purpose) rarely change. Our *how* (our mission) changes every day. Don't confuse these three things.

"I don't know where to start looking." This is an honest answer that shines light on the problem with finding our purpose.

Most of us haven't found our purpose because we've been lied to our entire lives. The biggest lie about purpose is that we have to go on some nebulous search for it. The biggest truth about purpose is this: we choose it.

We choose our purpose by activating our black sheep; purpose comes from the animation of our core values. I believe we all have what I like to call a "flock of five," that is, a group of five black sheep values that we can care for and honor with deliberate intention on a daily basis. Here's my flock:

Creativity
Hope
Impact
Empathy
Family
Authenticity

First off, I know that's a list of six. I'm a rock star—we do everything to excess. I refer to a flock of five, but many of us may have one more or one less.

Later, I will outline the process of discovering your black sheep values and proving they are real. For now, know that once you have identified your honest-to-goodness black sheep, you can use them to choose your purpose.

My purpose, the reason I get up every day, is this: *To creatively impact people's lives by authentically providing hope.*

If you look closely, you will see four of my six black sheep activated within my statement of purpose: creativity, impact, authenticity and hope. My other two core values, empathy and family, are equally part of my authentic self. Anyone who knows me understands that my family is paramount in my life, and my own trials have given me an incredible amount of empathy for those suffering.

Turning your core values into action with a statement of purpose allows you to be deliberate with your intention. Discovering your black sheep values and choosing your purpose provides a framework for achieving success. It enables you to choose *how* you engage with the world around you.

We all have a duty to engage with the world and lead others—whether they're family, friends, coworkers or even strangers—toward their own core values, purpose and mission.

LEADING ON PURPOSE

Most of us spend the majority of our lives in our day jobs, so we can all benefit from knowing how to lead with purpose at work.

Many organizations I work with struggle to engage their employees. They try all the usual suspects: bonuses, commissions, awards, vacations and so on, but still have trouble holding on to top talent. One of the main reasons people leave is a lack of alignment. Every day, employees try to align what matters most to them with what matters most to the organization. This is a potentially frustrating endeavor for a few reasons.

If employees haven't discovered their individual black sheep values, they will be trying to align with a moving target. Even if

High-performing teams use deliberate intention to align personal and organizational values.

When people contribute through their black sheep values, their unique purpose is amplified.

their organization's values are written in stone, constantly changing personal lists of what's important wreak havoc on the ability to align with the broader company vision. This can lead to feelings of unworthiness and instability on the employees' part.

To lead on purpose, not only do you have to know what your black sheep values are, you have to help those you lead to find theirs. In doing so, you present the best opportunity for people to feel like they are valued members of the team and are doing what they are meant to do.

For example, let's say your organization's core values are integrity, transparency, flexibility and diversity, and your black sheep values are honesty, communication, perseverance, loyalty and courage. You need to look at each of your company's core values and apply your black sheep to potential solutions. How would you *honestly* show transparency? Perhaps it would take *courage* to promote diversity in your department. You might *loyally* be flexible in your approach to leading your team ... By reviewing each organizational value through the lens of your black sheep values, you bring more of your best self to the table. Then, you must encourage your people to follow the same process with their own core values.

When someone contributes with deliberate intention (in other words, through their black sheep) and they can see their impact on the work at hand, their unique purpose within the organization is amplified. The results are reduced turnover, increased innovation, more productivity and, most important, happier employees.

The positive ripple effect on company culture can inspire others throughout the organization.

Unfortunately, investing in helping employees discover their core values is often looked at as a soft skill, and not one that influences the bottom line. Companies would rather invest in building the key performance indicator–friendly hard skills needed to do the job. If you wonder why top talent is leaving, it's because they think their company doesn't care about what truly matters to them.

If an organization's professed core values can't be seen in the real world, it is incredibly difficult for employees to align with anything. If a company declares transparency as a core value and yet hides important information from its employees, it upsets teams. It feeds a "feelings monster" that leads to negative behaviors like water-cooler griping. Leaders are responsible for knowing the organization's black sheep values that create the environment for employees to work within.

Core values are sacred. For individuals, they are held most dear; they are the literal non-negotiables. People expect their organizations to give their core values that level of importance as well. When an organization disrespects its core values, its people take it personally: *If the company doesn't care about its own values, why will it care about mine?* Exit stage left.

If you are a leader of an organization, make sure your company looks at its black sheep values and seeks proof that they are real. Without proof, the values don't exist. Without proof, there can be no commitment. Without proof, top talent leaves.

Your black sheep inform your purpose, and your purpose fuels your commitment to action.

LEADING YOUR LIFE ON PURPOSE

Using purpose to drive toward goals works well beyond the corporate world. Purpose can keep you committed to your personal goals in an incredibly powerful way.

Take Bob, who has a goal of losing forty pounds. Bob has done the work and discovered that his black sheep are these:

Compassion

Connection

Health

Faith

Love

By activating his black sheep he has chosen a purpose: "To compassionately love others through a healthy lifestyle and powerful faith in God."

When Bob's alarm goes off at 5:30 in the morning, and it's time for him to go to the gym, the tug-of-war between his values and feelings is in full effect over his warmly snuggled body in his super-comfortable bed. In similar situations, some of us have feelings that scream, *Piss off!* (In this case, we feel angry that we didn't get enough sleep.) Others have more devious, seductive feelings that say, *You have a big day ahead and need to be well-rested to perform your best. Take another thirty minutes.*

In those moments, we can look to our black sheep values to counterbalance our feelings. Bob can acknowledge that he is tired and would love to sleep in, but that one of his core values is health, and he truly wants to lose some weight. The productive tension is back. Rather than let either the value or his feelings win, Bob can look to his purpose for the commitment he needs to roll out of bed.

How does his purpose inspire commitment? It reminds Bob that going to the gym will make him feel better, which will make it easier for him to compassionately love others through a healthy lifestyle and to be a powerful witness of his faith.

So Bob drags himself out of bed, asks God for the ability to be a powerful witness and heads to the gym with deliberate intention. He doesn't do it to get healthy. He does it to fulfill his purpose. That is how you stay committed to your goals.

"SHEEP THRILLS" REMINDER

What: Your purpose isn't a mysterious entity hiding within you. Your purpose is a tool for engaging your core values, and you can choose to pick it up and use it every day.

Why: A life lived on purpose drives you toward achieving your goals.

How: Begin to own the five values that are most important to you. Notice when you act on them and actively look for opportunities to show them to the people around you.

The search for your black sheep can be an emotional, sometimes painful journey. Most people don't start this quest with a clear picture of who they are. To find your undiscovered self, you must face uncertainty and an inherently uncomfortable level of vulnerability. The first step in separating who you'd prefer to see yourself as from who you actually are is to have a bone-crushingly honest conversation with yourself. This requires some reliving of the past, which can be agonizing at times. But when you're devastatingly truthful about who you really are, you can affirm your black sheep in the present—and that's a step toward being fully you.

4

A BONE-CRUSHINGLY HONEST CONVERSATION

Vulnerability sucks.

LOVE BRENÉ BROWN. There, I said it. This alpha male, don't-cry, trash-talking guy's guy loves the queen of vulnerability and shame. I don't just love her... she is like my spirit animal. Her work has transformed my ability to communicate, and the depth of her platform is what I aspire to build one day.

The change Brené Brown has created in this world is legacy-worthy. If you haven't read any of her books, stop reading this one, go read *Daring Greatly* and then return to these pages. A research professor at the University of Houston, Brown is equal parts mind-blowingly brilliant and captivatingly relatable. It's a powerful combination. Her Netflix special *The Call to Courage* is a genre-busting opus that showcases her ability to convey powerful truths in a pull-up-a-stool-and-have-a-beer-with-me kind of way. Her work on embracing vulnerability as a strength is changing the face of leadership as we know it. Brown names the three qualities of vulnerability:

Uncertainty

Risk

Emotional exposure

The fear of these three elements stands in the way of you finding your black sheep. But you'll need all of them to have a bone-crushingly honest conversation with yourself. Sometimes the things that matter most to you are not born from happy memories. To discover your true core values, you are going to have to take a good look at yourself before you can go forward. Why is it so hard? Because, like accountability, vulnerability sucks.

The ancient Chinese philosopher Lao-tzu said, "If you are depressed you are living in the past. If you are anxious you are living in the future. If you are at peace you are living in the present." This is the perfect place to start our conversation. Generally, when I first start working with people to find their black sheep, the initial five that they identify are not what we end up with at the end of the journey. Lao-tzu's quote sheds some light on why.

The mountain of self-awareness is a slippery slope to climb. When you first identify your black sheep, you are likely to name two or three core values that are present and provable, and two or three that aren't real for you. They are what I call "aspirational values" that represent who you want to be rather than who you actually are. This is where the emotional exposure aspect of vulnerability comes into play. It is surprisingly difficult to discover what matters most. You've got to look deep and comb through your past for the powerful experiences that have molded you. During the process, you have to battle your insecurities and put aside what everyone else in the world tells you that you should care about.

For example, Kathy is a smoker. She has smoked for forty years. She knows it isn't good for her and, in the past, she has tried unsuccessfully to quit. She has endured her children confronting her with questions like "Don't you want to see you granddaughter graduate from high school and get married?" Because of that, when she digs for her non-negotiables, she chooses health as one of her values and hopes it will help her quit smoking.

It's an understandable approach—but it won't work. When Kathy is bone-crushingly honest with herself, she admits that she has lived a tough life and, though she hopes to live on, being around twenty years from now isn't a goal of hers. Health isn't one of her black sheep at all. That is a really difficult conversation to have with yourself, never mind with one of your children. If you feel ashamed about your truth, that might confuse you about which black sheep are truly yours. So keep in mind, you're not doing this to please anyone else, and it won't work to try. Your truth is *yours* and no one else's. The key to success is to get real about who you are in the present. It's the only way.

Here's the thing: *Black sheep don't live in the future.*

Remember, our core values are formed over the course of our lives; they rarely change and they serve as a powerful anchor to keep us in the present. By the time we are out on our own, most of us have lived enough life to form what matters most to us. But instead of diving deep when we are young, we wait till we become a depression-filled forty-something to begin to ask if we are happy with who we are and if we're doing what we are meant to do. We make decades' worth of uniformed decisions with less than positive consequences.

Enter Brené Brown's work on shame. Sometimes the things that shape us when we are younger are attached to some sort of shame. It's a powerful emotion that can disrupt the healthy tension between our values and our feelings. Because shame hurts, it stops us from looking deep within ourselves. This can lead to crippling depression.

To fight that pain, we often craft a narrative about being the person we long to be instead of accepting who we are. We might even pretend to be someone we aren't. We imagine ourselves in the future and convince ourselves *that person* is who we are in the present. But that person is not real.

The crazy thing is, we project this fake persona outward for the world to see because we are afraid of who we *might* be. What's wrong with who we are? When we scare ourselves out of discovering who we truly are because we think we won't be able to handle what we might find, we can't answer that question. What are we so afraid of?

Uncertainty. Uncertainty and vulnerability work together to create fear. It's biological. Our brains are factory-wired to view

Take a hard-core look at who you are— not who you wish you were, definitely not who others would like you to be.

uncertainty as a threat. How do you feel when threatened? Fearful? Of course you do! If that is the case and you know your brain will react with fear, then you overcome it by using your black sheep values as a guidepost when facing the unknown. The irony is that facing the things that make you afraid allows you to overcome the fear. (Eat your heart out, Alanis Morissette!)

Most of us don't want to endure that uncertainty. So we stop looking at it. We accept our place in the flock of white sheep and go about our lives.

YOU WERE MEANT FOR MORE

I believe, with every part of my being, that *you were meant for more*. Building up the courage to push through and find your black sheep values empowers you to use deliberate intention to achieve everything you've ever wanted. You will stop winging it and start creating the impact you were meant to. You will start living the life you've only dreamed of until now. It's right in front of you. There is only one "F'n" obstacle in your way.

> **Feelings?** Nope.
> **Fear?** Nay.
> **Fortitude?** Check out the big brain on Brad! Uh ... no.
> **F*ck.** Settle down.
> Try: **Forgiveness.** Or lack of it.

Forgiveness may be the single most powerful thing on the planet. Learning to give and accept forgiveness is key in your journey to uncovering your black sheep. Until you learn to see the beauty in an imperfect world, your expectation of perfection will taint your ability to have an honest conversation. So let's start with forgiving yourself.

Have you ever screwed up so badly that the very idea of forgiving yourself makes you angry? You tell yourself that you don't deserve forgiveness. The self-blame lingers for what seems like forever. It rears its head at the worst moments. It's your kryptonite.

My father, Ted, often offers an endearing piece of advice that applies here. It is one of his favorite sayings, basically his Swiss Army knife of phrases: *Cut the shit*.

"Dad, I'm standing in the New England Patriots' locker room!"
"Cut the shit!" (amazement)

"Dad, Trump just got elected."
"Cut the shit!" (disbelief)

"Dad, I don't think I'm good enough to do this."
"Cut the shit!" (disagreement)

Our culture's obsession with perfection has infected our ability to be reasonable. It demands that we satisfy everyone's expectations of us rather than let us simply be who we are. We end up

Learn to forgive yourself by forgiving someone else first.

trying to hold ourselves up to an impossible standard, and we fail. Because we are human. I get it.

It took me a long time to get over letting those doctors convince me that my son was going to die. I couldn't forgive myself for years. I had to take a deep look at the situation, in retrospect, to understand what had happened: If I hadn't believed the doctors, I wouldn't have called my brother so that he could say his good-byes. My brother wouldn't have made the video that went viral. Five hundred thousand people wouldn't have looked for an answer, and Theo wouldn't have survived. I wouldn't have felt the agony of believing I'd given up on him, and I wouldn't have asked why I gave up and have seen that it was because I hadn't defined my core values. So, ultimately, I wouldn't have made it my life's work to help others find their black sheep, and I most certainly wouldn't have written this book. In a way, you are reading these words because I learned to forgive. But it wasn't me who I forgave first.

In the Gospel of Matthew, we are told that our ability to be forgiven begins with our capacity to forgive others. Although this might sound blasphemous, I discovered that I had to forgive God for what had happened to Theo. I didn't understand why my son had to suffer so much. I still don't. But the value *hope* is one of my black sheep, and hope and forgiveness are interdependent. I knew that to forgive myself, I had to repair my relationship with Him. Once I was able to forgive God for what seemed like the senseless suffering of my son, I could find it in me to forgive myself for my shortcomings in the face of that suffering.

Self-forgiveness is a complex and ongoing process that requires constant care. I turned to my faith to understand how to forgive myself. I don't know what you believe, but I do know this: *You deserve forgiveness.* Whatever you are holding on to that stops you from forgiving yourself, cut the shit!

VULNERABLE AND UNBREAKABLE

Being vulnerable makes us want to build unbreakable walls around ourselves. We spend years protecting ourselves from anything that could harm us. We compartmentalize and stuff issues into tiny emotional boxes and bury them deep inside, waiting for a timely Thanksgiving-dinner moment for everything to bubble over and come flying out in a fury of nonsensical logic. *I hate this cranberry sauce! You've resented my success for the last ten years! And stop blaming the dog for that putrid smell—we know it's you!*

Can you be vulnerable *and* unbreakable? I think so. A few years ago I came across something called Kintsugi. Kintsugi is an ancient Japanese philosophy and process of repairing broken pottery. The legend says that in the late fifteenth century, Japanese shogun Ashikaga Yoshimasa sent his favorite tea bowl, which was broken, back to China to be repaired. It returned with ugly metal staples in it, and the shogun was less than pleased. So he sent it out to

The secret to becoming unbreakable is realizing that you are already broken. We all are.

some local artisans and told them to fix it. Rather than try to make the teapot look like it had never been broken, the artisans used the most valuable resource at their disposal—gold—to repair the cracks. By doing so, they not only increased the value of the bowl with the beautiful designs the gold created while bonding the broken pieces together, but they also showcased its history. *Kintsugi* translates as "golden repair."

Perhaps you have spent far too much time and energy trying to protect yourself from the things that could break you rather than focusing on what's holding your brokenness together: those five core values that make you, you. Just as gold was the most valuable material the local artisans could find to repair the bowl, your black sheep are your most valuable resource. They are the glue that holds your brokenness together. Use them to do the following:

Refine you. With your black sheep, you focus on your five non-negotiables rather than the dozens of things that are merely "important." This simplified perspective allows you to balance in the tug-of-war between your emotions and your black sheep values so that you make good decisions.

Empower you. When you deliberately act from the place of your values, you control the narrative in front of you to positively impact the situation at hand. Your black sheep are designed to be illuminated! They should be the first thing people see within you and the first thing you look to when you are struggling.

Connect you. When you do the work to discover what matters most to you, you find that you are not alone. Many people share the same values and face the same challenges that you do. Knowing that we are all in this together provides a comfort that helps you share and be more vulnerable.

If you aren't using your black sheep to hold your brokenness together, what *are* you using? Emotions? Ideas? Wishes? I can't answer the question for you. I can tell you that to stop winging it, you've got to find and care for your black sheep. They are the rock-solid foundation from which to move toward your goals.

"SHEEP THRILLS" REMINDER

What: Get vulnerable, and ferociously honest, about who you are and what matters most to you.

Why: In being exactly who you are—including showing the places where you're broken—you will deeply connect with others and influence them.

How: Have faith that your black sheep will hold you together, especially at the times and in the places where you feel you might fall apart.

You have favorites for a reason. The joy of listening to your favorite song on the radio or watching your favorite movie on TV goes far beyond the fact that you love them. Despite the strong emotions these things conjure, most people rarely ask themselves why a favorite makes them feel so good. Favorites connect you with the deep-rooted values born from powerful experiences that you have had over the course of your life.

5

PLAYING FAVORITES

Powerful experiences form your core values.

COMEDIAN BRIAN REGAN has a hilarious routine about playing Little League baseball as a child and being awful at it. He recounts a story of playing in the outfield and not really paying attention to the game. He was there to get a free sno-cone after the final inning. When a teammate yelled to Brian and asked the score, Brian yelled back "Grape!" and proceeded to tell him that grape and cherry were his favorite flavors.

That routine makes me laugh every time I hear it, for a few reasons. I have coached players who are more interested in picking flowers in the grass than the game at hand ... and I also happen to love grape. It is one of my favorite flavors, whether it's grape juice, grape jelly, Grimace ... hell, I even love the color purple and the Purple One himself—Prince!

Despite its detractors, I still believe that *Purple Rain* is an underappreciated film classic, and the title track is my favorite song ever written. I hear it and I am instantly transported to slow dancing at my junior high school semi-formal, with a beautiful girl that I was head over heels for. I was so nervous that I was going to screw something up that, to this day, when "Purple Rain" comes on my car radio, my palms start sweating! I remember what I call "The Kiss" (my first "galoche," if you know what I mean). The awful, awkward, tongue-twisting mess was like the drool-filled love of a well-intentioned Saint Bernard. I had no idea what I was doing. I wanted to be a good kisser but I hadn't the slightest idea of how to figure it out, as the wonderful world of the internet hadn't been invented yet.

Why do I tell you all this? The point is, your favorites are grounded in the deep-rooted memories and experiences attached to them, just as "Purple Rain" is for me. Today, I feel empathy for my struggling fourteen-year-old self, and that same empathy manifests for those who search for the undiscovered answers to living their best life.

Your favorites are connected to what Maslow would call "peak experiences," and they usually reflect one or more of your core values. So looking at what you consider a favorite becomes a fascinating study. Let's consider your favorite movie for a minute. What is one of your top three favorite movies of all time, one that when it randomly comes on the television, you simply can't turn off? *Showgirls*? I get it. (If, indeed, your answer was *Showgirls*, I will make myself available for a free counseling session when you finish this book.) Having asked that question to thousands of people, the top two answers are *The Shawshank Redemption* and *The Princess Bride.*

One of my favorite movies of all time is *Happy Gilmore*. That should explain much of what you have questioned about me up to now. The Adam Sandler golf parody is a lowbrow, idiotic comedy classic—and I love it. When I first asked myself why it is one of my favorites, I assumed the answer was because of the type of humor it portrays, or perhaps because Sandler and I are from the same hometown and I simply feel some love for a local boy who's done well. That all changed when I examined the movie through the lens of my black sheep. As you know, my six black sheep values are creativity, hope, impact, empathy, family and authenticity. With those in mind, let's look at why *Happy Gilmore* is one of my favorites:

Creativity: Have you seen Happy hit a golf ball? Have you ever tried to hit a golf ball like Happy does? Of course you have. Running up to the ball and taking an out-of-control, mighty swing at that little round white ghost has made many a Peppermint Patty laugh at your Charlie Brown moment. Would you consider that swing creative? Uh...yes.

Hope: All Happy wanted to do with his life was to become a professional hockey player. In spite of a wicked slap shot and his ability to fight, he never made it. The day after his failed tryout, he stands in a batting cage taking baseballs off his head to toughen up before next year's tryouts. All I wanted to be growing up was a professional baseball player. Despite having the necessary skills, I got hurt and my injury threatened my only childhood dream. I understand what it's like to hold on to hope for something you have wished for, for so long.

Impact: When Happy joins the PGA Tour, people in cut-off jean shorts and beer helmets start to show up at the golf matches. He attracts the everyman with his down-to-earth persona and blatant disregard for the rules of golf. There is something so defiant and attractive in that to me. That's the type of impact I aim to have. I work to make living a life of fulfillment with deliberate intention accessible to everyone.

Empathy: Watching Happy fail at his dream conjures up some serious feelings for me. When I say I wanted to play professional baseball, what I mean is that I had no backup plan. It was all or nothing. When the truth of my situation turned baseball reality into "nothing" for me, my entire life turned upside down. I've walked a mile in those shoes and it sucks. Happy has success in a sport he doesn't want to play: golf. I empathize with his need to succeed in the only thing that matters to him: hockey.

Family: Happy joins the PGA Tour to win enough money to purchase his grandmother's house, which his grandfather built with his bare hands. The IRS has taken it because of unpaid taxes. Happy sets his grandmother up in a temporary retirement home while he earns the money to buy back her house at auction. He wants to save his family… I think we can agree that it's obvious why this resonates with me.

Authenticity: In one of my favorite scenes in the movie, Happy asks out the PGA Tour's publicity agent Virginia Venit, played by Julie Bowen, on a date. She tells Happy that she doesn't date golfers, to which he replies, "Good, because I'm a hockey player." Happy knows who he is, in spite of the job he performs to accomplish a goal. That level of authenticity is what I aspire to every day.

On the surface, the stupid humor and hometown connection could pass for why *Happy Gilmore* is one of my favorite movies. Looking at it more closely, however, the movie checks the box of each of my core values. It feeds all the black sheep in my care. It connects me to past experiences that profoundly impacted me and brings a smile to my face. Of course it would be a favorite!

I invite you to use favorites to begin the journey of finding your black sheep. This is a fun, low-risk way to start asking yourself some deeper, and potentially difficult, questions. Take a few moments to answer the following questions. I recommend writing your answers down in a journal or on a device where you keep notes. You won't dive in too deep yet. For now, let's just figure out what some of your favorites actually are.

What are your top three favorite movies?

What are the themes of these movies?

Are there particular characters who resonate with you?

What do they remind you of?

What are your top three favorite songs?

What are the themes of these songs?

Do you attach a specific memory to the songs when you hear them?

What do they remind you of?

What are your top three favorite foods?

When did you first get introduced to these foods?

Did someone close to you make these foods for you?

What do they remind you of?

What are your top three favorite smells?

What is your earliest memory of these smells?

Who is attached to the memories?

What do they remind you of?

Examining your favorite movies, songs, foods and smells will reveal some hidden truths about what matters most to you. But don't overanalyze your answers right now. Write down your first thoughts and, eventually, you will come back to them for evidence of your black sheep.

When I'm working with people, I'm sometimes asked: "What if I don't have any favorites?" You might be wondering the same

**Think of your
black sheep as your
own personal hit
song that connects
your head and
your heart.**

thing. Just as trying to focus on lots of things that are important to you can muddy the truth of what matters most, identifying lots of things you like blurs the image of your favorites. My advice is to ask yourself: *If I could watch only one movie... listen to only one song... eat only one meal... what would it be?*

This isn't about right or wrong answers. It's about getting to the truth. Sometimes you have to work your way through this process several times. Choose something that feels right and if, later on, you realize that you have a different favorite, so be it. The process is what's important.

IT'S NOT JUST *WHAT*, IT'S *WHO*

As you search for your black sheep, examine not just *what* is most important to you, but also *who* you surround yourself with. This is incredibly important. The ability to reveal your black sheep when and where you desire can be powerfully impacted by the people who influence you.

I cohost a popular thirty-minute podcast called *Thoughts That Rock* with one of my best friends and mentors, Jim Knight. Jim is a former Hard Rock International executive, the best-selling author of *Culture That Rocks* and one of the most popular speakers in the country. On our podcast we ask our guests one simple question: "What is the best advice you have ever been given?"

In a recent episode, we interviewed Don Yaeger, an eleven-time *New York Times*–best-selling author, award-winning journalist for *Sports Illustrated* and revered business coach. Don had the extraordinary opportunity to be mentored for more than a decade by legendary UCLA basketball coach and leadership guru John Wooden. The episode is worth a listen for the story of how Wooden became one of Yaeger's mentors alone, but the advice Wooden gave Yaeger knocked our socks off. One of the biggest lessons he learned from Coach Wooden was: *You will never outperform your inner circle. If you want to know what the capacity of your success is, look at your inner circle.*

Wow! Think about the implications of that advice on your internal and external realities. Internally, you can think of your black sheep as forming your inner circle. You will perform at the highest levels, on purpose, when you engage and empower them. Externally, you must look at who you spend the most time with. Coach Wooden suggests separating your people into three categories:

Personal contacts: Which five people do you spend the most time with in your personal life?

Professional contacts: Which five people do you spend the most time with in your work life?

Other contacts: Which five people do you spend the most time with in other activities you are involved with (your church, volunteer or leisure activities and so on)?

Make sure your relationships are worth the investment.

Wooden had Yaeger review all fifteen people he identified and asked him one question: "Are they going where you are going?"

Do your people encourage you? Are they part of what you want to achieve or are they holding you back? If every interaction with someone is filled with drama and challenges, my advice is to let them go. One of the most difficult lessons a great leader will learn is that sometimes the people who got you to where you are, are not the people to take you where you want to go.

A challenging and potentially painful process of pruning the relationships in your life follows this realization. You might need to redistribute your time to those who are headed in the direction of your ultimate goals. When you look at what and who is guiding you, think about both your black sheep values and your inner circle. Make sure that your relationships with both are real and worth the investment.

"SHEEP THRILLS" REMINDER

What: Your favorites affirm your core values.

Why: Like your favorites, your black sheep are where your head and your heart connect.

How: Look at what you love and ask yourself what values you see there.

How do you know if the black sheep you've identified are really yours? You need proof. In this initial search for truth, most people discover at least a few values that are merely important to them masquerading as those five non-negotiables. You have to dig through your daily life in search of evidence that your black sheep are alive and well in the present. Remember, black sheep don't live in the future.

6

DIGGING FOR TRUTH

The fastest way to lose your black sheep is to get distracted by what's merely important to you.

USED TO suffer from crippling anxiety. Once Theo "survived" his battle with cancer, I spent much of my time living in the magical Land of What Ifs in the town of Futureville. I spent most of my days worrying about what could happen or how we were going to pay for continued treatment or how we were going to manage the aftercare *and* raise our other child.

When you survive something like cancer, people think the war has been won. All the support you received during the darkest hours dissipates. The meal trains slow down, the number of prayers for you dwindle and the extra hands that were *everywhere* when you were in the hospital go away. People don't understand that you still have many, many battles to fight. It becomes overwhelming to try to honor all the things that are now incredibly important. The 870-pound gorilla and reigning champion of the world of disorders—anxiety—enters the ring with one goal: to beat your ass.

An estimated 284 million people worldwide have experienced an anxiety disorder, making it the most prevalent mental health disorder around the globe. Anxiety affects nearly 30 percent of all adults at some point in their lives, with women being twice as likely to be afflicted with it than men. The only way I could prepare myself to battle this ugly disease was to find and care for my black sheep. It's incredibly distracting to chase emotional squirrels around in your head. If you know what matters most in your life, you can focus on those five simple, transformative values and let go of everything else that doesn't serve you.

Using your favorites to help you confirm your flock of five, as you did in the last chapter, is only the beginning. The next step requires some vulnerability, honesty and commitment. Separating what you find really important from your true non-negotiables takes time, exploration and proof. When I conduct workshops to help people discover their black sheep values, to get started we use a worksheet that lists about 120 different, commonly held core values, such as these:

Accuracy	Generosity	Respect
Beauty	Innovation	Results
Community	Justice	Service
Determination	Kindness	Tradition
Diversity	Meaning	Wealth
Education	Optimism	Well-being
Freedom	Power	

You can grab a copy of that worksheet with the full list, for yourself, downloadable for free at www.findyourblacksheep.com.

The worksheet is designed to get you first to identify the values that you consider important. When I ask participants to circle every value that resonates with them, they usually circle somewhere between twenty and thirty words. This is completely normal—and also the root of the problem.

It's impossible to consistently honor and engage with that many values every day. But that is exactly where most of us start. We set ourselves up for failure when we haven't separated our black sheep values from the things we deem merely important in our lives. Consciously or unconsciously, we try to honor values numbering in the double digits, and we fail to manifest the change we seek... and we feel bad about it... and we beat ourselves up over it... and even though, deep down, we know we can't win, we keep trying... and the cycle continues. *You've got to break the cycle!*

This cycle mirrors the situation that farmers find themselves in, trying to care for hundreds of sheep that are all equally important and hard to separate from one another. How do they overcome that challenge? They place one black sheep to serve as a marker for every hundred white sheep in their flock. Rather than focusing on the large group of sheep in front of them, they focus on the black sheep to alert them to potential danger.

To break the cycle, you need to do the same thing with your core values. You have to find the five black sheep values among the twenty or thirty things that are merely important to you.

As you chip away at finding your honest-to-goodness, dyed-in-the-wool black sheep values, you come closer to your undiscovered, authentic self.

Group the words you circled on your worksheet into similar categories. Words like *empathy* and *sympathy* are of the same likeness and go together. *Community* and *relationships, faith* and *spirituality, accomplishment* and *success, accountability* and *reliability*... you get the idea. By doing this, you create five buckets of similar words. Choose one word (the most important one, the one you cannot live without) from each bucket to arrive at an initial five core values that you can work with. Your list could look something like this:

**Accountability, adventure, connection, self-awareness, hope
Commitment, discipline, reliability, loyalty, happiness
Faith, health, trust, stability, creativity**

Or any other combination of five core values that speak to you.

Having identified what you think are your flock of five, return to the work you did on your favorites. Are you ready to have some fun? I hope you are, because I'm about to assign some homework.

The first thing I want you to do over the next week or so is to watch your three favorite movies with deliberate intention. Follow these guidelines:

Note when your black sheep appear. As you watch each movie, keep a list of your flock of five next to you. Every time you see one of your five black sheep exhibited on-screen, place a check mark next to it.

Review your results. When you've finish watching the movies, review how many times your black sheep showed up. Did any of them appear more than others? If two or three appeared more often, it strongly suggests that those particular black sheep indeed belong to you.

Evaluate the evidence. Notice if any of the five values you initially listed didn't show up in your favorite movies at all. Remember, sometimes we select aspirations instead of what we truly value in the present. If some of your values appear rarely or don't show up at all, it could suggest that they are aspirational. At this point, simply identify when this happens, as it is a red flag that one of the initial black sheep you identified may not actually be yours.

Projecting the values that are most important to you onto the movie screen is a fun way to start a bone-crushingly honest conversation with yourself. You could do this exercise with any of the songs, food or smells you identified in the previous chapter. However, if you are going to get to the whole truth, you will also need to see precisely where your black sheep operate in real life.

To prove that your black sheep values exist in the real world, you have to consider your flock of five and channel your inner Indiana Jones for a bit of core values archaeology, including record-keeping, not just jumping from horses onto tanks at breakneck speed.

For a week, at the end of each day, before you go to bed, I want you to answer some questions in a journal. Write down your five core values, leaving space for documentation between each word. Below each word, record your responses to the following questions:

Did this black sheep show up today? How many times? A quick dig through your day will reveal if this black sheep manifested itself. Take note of every time it manifested, not just whether or not it did. The more the value shows up, the more proof you have that you own this black sheep.

What was the scenario? Document the scenario where your black sheep appeared. Look for patterns in how the value shows up. Does it appear when you are challenged? When you are given a platform to speak? When you feel safe? Documenting these patterns sheds some light on the scenarios you need to place yourself in to truly empower your black sheep.

With whom did it appear? Track who experiences your black sheep with you. Is it a trusted friend? A foe? A family member? By documenting who sees your black sheep, you will start to identify the types of people you surround yourself with. This will help you construct a trusted inner circle.

At the end of the week, you will have collected some significant data related to the truth you are looking for. If you are like most of the people I work with, you will find that two or three of the values you initially identified show up every day, consistently. Often these are some of the most deeply rooted core values you possess. They are the ones that you could have figured out without any of the exercises, because you just feel it in your gut. It's good to confirm that these values belong to you—they're part of what makes you extraordinary. But what about the other two or three that haven't yet shown up consistently?

THREE STEADYING QUESTIONS

When you discover that you listed a few values that don't show up with the frequency you expected during your week of tracking, ask yourself three more questions:

> **Are these values actually my black sheep, or are they just something that I feel is important?**
>
> **Are these values aspirational rather than representative of who I am in the present?**
>
> **Am I sabotaging myself so that these values don't appear?**

In the case of the first question, sometimes the "important" words are too narrow and you need to level up to a bigger, more encompassing word to find your black sheep. For example, let's say that Chris listed relationships, faith and family as three of his core

Are you caring for someone else's sheep?

values. When he tried to track these values, they sort of blended into each other, and when he journaled about them, it was difficult to separate them. In a case like this, I would encourage Chris to level up and look for a word like *connection*, which could encompass relationships, faith and family.

It works like this: What Chris values most about his relationships with his friends, coworkers and others is that he creates meaningful *connection* with a wide circle of high-achievers. With his faith (Buddhism), he values the *connection* with principles of service, morals and ethics. He deeply values his *connection* with his spouse, brothers, sisters, parents, grandparents and extended family. By leveling up to a single, more accessible word, Chris can accurately track his black sheep and select two more that he will test, prove and then deliberately express more of in the world.

In the case of the second question above, about aspirational values, when you start your search for your black sheep, it's completely normal to write down one or more that you think you *should* care about rather than what you *actually* care about. Self-awareness takes practice, vulnerability and honesty. If the black sheep you identified don't appear in your life at all, it's a good sign that they are a projection of your *should*, rather than the you who, I promise, is awe-inspiring just as you are. But to authentically express that in the world, you need to discover who you truly are first.

As for the third question, when it comes to self-sabotage, you need to see if you are doing something to stop your black sheep from manifesting themselves. Having balanced, thoughtful responses to life can be a real challenge if you let your feelings win the tug-of-war with your core values. Remember that a good decision is one that is born from your values, considers all the facts and honors what you are feeling in the moment—but it doesn't let your feelings take over. Make sure you recognize and acknowledge your feelings when you're having them. If you are overly upset or consumed by anger, these emotions might get in the way of your values appearing.

After the first week of tracking, adjust your core values by leveling them up, being honest and tweaking them to be as accurate as possible. Then track them for an additional week. By the end of the second week, you should have significant proof that the black sheep you identified are indeed in your flock.

Caring for your black sheep is a daily choice. There will be days when you don't feel like doing the work. That's okay. You don't have to seek perfection. What you want is the strongest commitment you can conjure at any given moment. That's why finding your black sheep is so important. On the days when you don't feel like doing something, your black sheep hold you accountable to trying. They remind you to ask yourself what matters most, so you can be the best steward of the limited energy you may have to give on a bad day. Rather than blindly spending your energy on things that won't move the needle in your life, you can refocus through your flock of five and make sure you create alignment on purpose.

Authenticity is impossible if your black sheep are lost.

NOW YOU GET TO *WHY*

Once you have found your black sheep and proven they are real, you can finally take control of your life by making another decision: choosing your purpose.

As we talked about in chapter 3, your purpose represents the activation of your core values. Your purpose is your *why*, and it aligns with what matters most to you. I encourage you to write a simple statement of purpose that you refer to often.

Here's how it looks. Rachel's black sheep are the following:

Connection

Trust

Empathy

Authenticity

Creativity

She brings these black sheep to life with a statement of purpose: "To positively connect with others, building trust through creative and authentic self-expression."

See how her purpose encompasses four of her five core values? If you can include all of your values in your purpose without trying too hard to make it fit, go for it.

If you had started with *why* (your purpose) before you identified your black sheep, how many of your values do you think would appear in it? If any did, it would be by dumb luck or by accident.

That's not living with deliberate intention. You need to know what matters most in order to honor that and live the life of fulfillment you desire. So, let's do this...

List your black sheep below:

_____

_____

_____

_____

Incorporating as many of your black sheep as makes sense, craft your simple statement of purpose.

My purpose is: _____

Can we pause for a minute? If you have done the work up to this point, stop and acknowledge that. You are officially part of the 1 percent! Not *that* 1 percent... I'm talking about the 1 percent of people who do the work to take control of their lives and start living with deliberate intention. You have defined your *what* and your *why*, and now you are ready to learn *how* to make your black sheep as real for others as they are for you. You are finally prepared to experience the transformation that this work creates. I am incredibly proud of you. Well done.

"SHEEP THRILLS" REMINDER

What: Evidence of what matters most to you *will* show up in your day.

Why: Black sheep are not aspirational. They're all about reality, and it's your job to prove to yourself that you're right about which black sheep are truly yours.

How: Write down your five core values and search for them in your daily activities.

Having found your black sheep and having proved they belong to you, you can release them into your life and let them lead. You can deliberately program them into your days with the intention that they be seen, felt and interacted with by everyone around you. Using your black sheep on purpose is the most powerful form of practical manifestation you will experience. You can literally speak your core values into existence, choosing when and where they show up. You can realize your purpose and live the life of fulfillment you were born for.

7

PRACTICAL MANIFESTATION

It's time for all missions possible.

N LATE 2018, in the span of three months, I had a personal revelation that would set in motion all of the work that I am doing today. In October I was asked to speak at Contract Forum. This event, hosted by *Contract* magazine, gathers the top designers in the country to talk about trends and where the interior design industry is going. They had asked me to speak about the importance of owning your core values in the design process.

I was so excited to give this talk to fellow artists and explain how our values factor into our work. I had planned on beginning my talk with this statement: "If you haven't defined your core values, you have never created an original design. Your complete body of work is merely a reflection of what other people care about."

I couldn't wait to drop that truth bomb on this crowd. I knew it would make them uncomfortable, and that is where we have to start—to accept that we are winging it. Before my session, another speaker opened the conference that morning. The organizers had asked Paula Zuccotti, a well-known product designer, ethnographer and trends forecaster to speak about her book, *Every Thing*

We Touch: A 24-Hour Inventory of Our Lives. Her book documents the lives of people of different ages, races, genders, religions, sexual orientations and so on, by capturing images of everything they touched during a period of twenty-four hours. Zuccotti laid out on the floor, in chronological order, all the objects the subjects put their hands on from the moment they woke up to the moment they went to bed, and snapped a single photograph per subject. In doing so, she gives us a glimpse into each person's day through stories told by the objects. It is *amazing*! She calls it "future archaeology"—predicting what matters most in people's lives based on the objects they engaged with.

I was riveted. I was enthralled. I was... panicking! During Zuccotti's incredible presentation, I asked myself one question: *If someone followed me around for twenty-four hours, would they see any evidence of my black sheep values?* The truth was... *maybe*... at best. This realization, that owning my black sheep was only part of a larger process, sent me spinning. It's incredibly important to define what matters most, but once you do that, what the hell happens next?

The answer came to me two months later in a *New York Times* article on entrepreneur, digital marketing guru, wine expert, best-selling author and in-your-freakin'-face internet sensation Gary Vaynerchuk. Vaynerchuk is the chairman of a New York–based communications company, VaynerX, and CEO of its subsidiary, VaynerMedia. GaryVee, as he is known to his fans, has one gigantic goal in life: to own the New York Jets. In the article, "The Self-Described Jets Owner-in-Waiting Will Tailgate for Now," journalist Zach Schonbrun interviews Gary's brother and business partner, AJ. Commenting on Gary's certainty about accomplishing his goal, AJ rocked my world, with five words: *He's speaking it into existence.*

And there it was. AJ just gave me the missing piece for practically manifesting our black sheep. Once we know what our five core values are, we need to *speak them into existence.* We need to choose when and where our black sheep appear and use them to control the narrative we create.

I began my journey of actively programming my black sheep into my day in January 2019. Over the course of ten months, my life transformed. My career skyrocketed, with triple the speaking engagements, a 200 percent increase in my speaking fees and doors opening at every turn to be a thought-leader in the core values/purpose space. My personal relationships have strengthened and incredible new people have entered my life, believing in the work I do, shouting it from the rooftops to their networks while whispering heartfelt encouragement into my ear. It's truly incredible.

With all this personal and professional success, it would be easy to set new goals and crush them one by one. However, it isn't about the goals. It isn't about the success. *It's about the process.*

Even GaryVee agrees. In a follow-up post to AJ's interview on www.garyvaynerchuk.com, Gary had this to say:

I don't care whether or not I end up buying the New York Jets. (And no, this has nothing to do with their current standing this season.)

The truth is, I just love the climb. I love the sweat, the long hours, the uncertainties, and the grind. Nothing in life comes easy, and when we're dealing with something as huge as a life-time goal, it's likely that things will change throughout that journey—but that's okay. It's part of the process. And that process is what I love so much.

I've said it a few times before—the day that I actually buy the Jets is going to make me incredibly upset, because the climb will be "over." That's what really worries me—Because, then what?...

It's not about the glory of reaching a personal goal, it's about the glory of relishing the journey and sharing in that accomplishment with those that helped us get there.

It's the last part of Vaynerchuk's statement that resonates with me so intensely. It's not about reaching the goal. It's about the process of achieving it and sharing the success with those we love. Speaking our black sheep into existence affects us—and everyone we come into contact with.

To lead with your black sheep, you have to be deliberate with your intention. You have to literally program them into your day. Pull out your calendar, review your schedule and decide where and when your black sheep will appear.

Black sheep are catalysts for transformational change.

It works like this: Let's say I have an appointment with Mary at 2 p.m. to discuss next month's marketing plan. I know that Mary is going through a difficult divorce and is struggling emotionally. I quickly survey my black sheep and realize that empathy and hope have the potential for powerful impact in Mary's life. So next to that two o'clock meeting, I write *empathy, hope* and *impact*. I am programming them to appear during our conversation. I am not going to rely on "a good moment" to show empathy or assume my values will show up by accident while I pat myself on the back for my thoughts of being helpful. I am deliberate with my intention and I choose to speak these black sheep values into existence.

Mary will see empathy and hope first, because I begin our meeting by saying something like: "Mary, I'm so sorry that you are going through this crap. It's incredibly difficult and I recognize that you are doing your best to manage. I want you to know that I will stand next to you through this in any way I can. I know it might be hard to see to this right now, but you are an amazing person and the positive impact you create in this organization says everything about who you are. If I can do anything to ease your stress over this, please let me know."

A few simple sentences to let Mary know she isn't alone. It doesn't seem like much on the surface, but anyone who has been in the quiet desperation of depression will tell you that a few simple words matter.

When you approach your day with deliberate intention, the control you have over your life is empowering. Let's say you have a dinner scheduled with your mother at seven in the evening. Ever since you lost your dad a few years ago, life has been difficult for her. Your mom is getting up there in age and you would really love for her to come live with you; however, she is an extremely proud woman and would never allow herself to be a burden to anyone. You have tried countless times to have a conversation about this with her and get very emotional in your plea to help, saying things like, "Mom, stop being so stubborn! I'm so frustrated. Why are you so unmovable about this?" You can't seem to make any progress.

You decide to try again at your scheduled dinner. But this time you program your black sheep to lead the way. For the sake of this example, let's say your black sheep are connection, gratitude, generosity, loyalty and trust. You go in with guns blazing and write all these words next to your 7 p.m. appointment. This time, the conversation goes differently: "Mom, I know we've had this discussion before and I understand your hesitation to agree. But I wanted you to understand why I'm asking. You raised me to be thankful for all that we have. You taught me to be generous with my time, my money and my heart. I watched you take a second job to help feed our family and you never let me feel like we had less than others. Your devotion to this family allowed me to trust you in everything you do. But now it's time for you to trust me. It's time for you to allow me to be generous and grateful. There is nothing I want more than to be a loyal daughter and have you close to me so I can help you like you have helped me. I'd love it if you'd reconsider and let me be the woman you raised me to be."

Speaking your core values into existence means planning how, where and with whom you will engage them every day.

Boom! Do you see the difference between leading with what matters most to you and an emotional plea for someone to acquiesce to what you want? Your mother might still say no. But if you honor all the things that matter most to you, you can feel good about your actions regardless of the outcome. When you speak your core values into existence, you resonate in a different way because your words are saturated with authenticity. They're real. They're honest. They're transformational.

Disclaimer: I like to believe that we all have an inherent good in us. But there is always the option to engage your values in a hurtful way. You could speak one of your values into existence with the explicit intent of doing harm to someone else. I have been asked, "What if one or more of my black sheep are assholes?" *Spoiler alert*: Your black sheep values can't be assholes... but you could be one, if that's what you want to be. Just know that if you choose to crush another person in service of achieving your values, you aren't honoring anything. In the words of the immortal Patrick Swayze in *Road House*, "Be nice."

Speaking your black sheep into existence is practical manifestation. I'm not a big believer in simply shouting your desires out loud so the universe can respond. I've always been turned off by all forms of the prosperity gospel. That's not what this is. In finding your black sheep, you connect to the deepest part of who you are. In defining what matters most, you can choose to act with deliberate intention, to honor those values in everything you do.

But your values aren't going to honor themselves. Pull up your calendar right now. Take a look at what you have scheduled for tomorrow. Ask yourself two questions:

> **Which black sheep would benefit the work I have to do? Where should my core values appear to help me achieve my goals?**

Go ahead and write them in next to your scheduled activities. Every activity is an opportunity for a small mission. This is how you are going to live out your purpose and honor your black sheep values. You can choose one or more values. Think through how you will use them. Make notes if necessary.

The goal is to be proactive and deliberate with your intention. It's your life on your terms. You are here to fulfill your purpose. You can do that by honoring your black sheep. Start training them to lead the way.

Your black sheep should be what people first see in you. They should provide the awareness that people need to help govern their behavior toward you. You have control over whether that happens or not. It's a choice.

Most people won't make that choice. Most people won't take the time to find their black sheep. Most people will settle for a life of winging it. It's gotten them this far… why change now?

You change now because you aren't experiencing life at its fullest. But something else is waiting for you. A life that will provide an unearthly sense of fulfillment. A life that aligns your purpose and your missions. This is what I want for you. I want you to wake up every day and look forward to letting your black sheep values lead. I want you to grab the pen and start writing your own story rather than letting everyone else take a turn. I want you to own your non-negotiables so that you can have spirited debate with others without letting your feelings cause problems. I want you to stop attaching your happiness to an outcome and start making good decisions that will move your life forward.

Above all, I want you to believe there is hope. There is hope that things can change. There is hope that even the things that feel impossible can be overcome. I've witnessed that miracle. I want to share that miracle with you. I hope you will accept it and experience it for yourself. Transformation awaits. The choice is yours.

"SHEEP THRILLS" REMINDER

What: Schedule your black sheep to appear throughout your day.

Why: Their appearance means you're activating your values and speaking your purpose into existence. This shows people what makes you uniquely you.

How: For each activity in your calendar, note which of your core values you will activate—and then make it happen.

Conclusion

CHANGE STARTS NOW

AS YOU embark on finding your black sheep, your perspective on the world around you will change. Things that used to drive you crazy will have significantly less effect on you. You will find yourself compelled by things that weren't even a consideration before. It's like being in the eye of a hurricane. A calmness grows in you as you recognize the amount of chaos swirling around you. That calmness can be unsettling. We are so used to living in the past or in the future that the present can be unrecognizable.

Your feelings will want to crash the party. They will want to suck you into the chaos. So you have to prepare yourself for when your feelings knock on your door. It would be great if they came obnoxiously crashing through the front entrance so you could recognize them for what they are. But they rarely do. They usually prefer to knock gently at the side entry and quietly cast doubt. They want to distract you long enough to make you stray from your core values. Your task is to keep the focus steady on your black sheep.

REAL CHANGE REQUIRES REAL WORK

Jim Trick is not only a successful life coach, an amazing singer/songwriter and a life-changing speaker, but he also holds one of the five spots in my inner circle. Jim is one of those people with a presence about him. A six-foot-tall Brazilian jujitsu student, with Buddy Holly glasses and a genuine curiosity that can make a brave soul blush, Jim commands attention. You'd be hard-pressed to walk around Marblehead, Massachusetts, and find someone who doesn't know him. His ability to make you feel like the only person in the room is why he never is.

Jim spent the majority of his life morbidly obese. At his heaviest, he was 430 pounds and had a sixty-six-inch waist. He describes a normal day of eating at that time: "[It] started with a breakfast of two bagels, one with extra butter and the other with extra cream cheese. Next, I stopped for an Egg McMuffin and two hash-brown patties. Once at the office, someone would say he was going to Dunkin' Donuts and would ask if I wanted anything. Hell, yeah, I did: a sausage, egg, and cheese bagel and a vat of coffee. Lunch was what most people had for dinner, and before dinner, I'd have a Double Whopper as a snack. If dinner was with friends, it was usually grilled chicken on a salad, with a side of whatever lie I was telling about my metabolism or thyroid."

It wasn't until Jim came home from work one night to find the electricity turned off that he had an epiphany. His financial life was as out of control as his eating. He had been out with friends

Beware the dangers of self-doubt.

and decided to end the day alone with a large pizza. As he sat in the dark, eating his pizza by flashlight, he finally felt the gravity of his situation. He needed help.

Jim decided to get gastric bypass surgery to help him drop some weight. Over the course of the next year, he was able to shed more than one hundred pounds. He felt great. He convinced himself the surgery was a magic bullet. It wasn't.

In spite of the surface progress he made, Jim never took the time to look inside for an anchor for his change. He began to fall back into bad habits and had nothing to hold himself accountable to. He began to hear dangerous whispers of self-doubt. "I had tried and failed so many times that the thought of trying again was off the table. I had resigned myself to the thought that this was just who I was and how I was going to be. And it wasn't just my weight that needed attention. I had a job that I was good at and paid well but drained my soul. My marriage was breaking down, and I had become generally dissatisfied with my life."

Not only did Jim listen to the whispers, he began to do the one thing that made him feel better... eat. Pound after pound returned as Jim's hope was looking for an exit. The bad choices that were destroying his life again led to an intervention by a close friend. That bone-crushingly honest conversation made Jim face his mortality. Luckily, the intervention worked.

Jim embarked on finding his core values. The journey led him to his five black sheep:

Compassionate connection

Impact

Health

Faith

Creativity

Over the next year, Jim began to speak his black sheep into existence. He entered counseling, began to work out, joined a jujitsu class, surrounded himself with his inner circle and decided to use his passion for food to create healthy dishes that honored what mattered most to him.

Along the way, the self-doubt came back with a vengeance. The pounds didn't melt away as easily as when he'd had the surgery. At every turn, Jim found himself battling the ghosts of his past. It was during this time that he figured out how to deal with his inner critic. As you begin to engage your black sheep, it's paramount to understand how to deal with your inner critic.

DRIVE THE BUS YOURSELF

Some will tell you to ignore your inner critic, to send them to the Phantom Zone like Superman did to General Zod. As enticing as that sounds, it doesn't work. You have to give your inner critic a voice. The fact is, amid all the negative shit they'll spew, your inner critic tells some important truths.

So rather than banish them, I suggest this: Picture yourself as a middle-school bus driver. You are heading to your destination and trying to control the chaos happening behind you. Your inner critic is like those obnoxious sixth graders trying to disrupt your attention and distract you from expertly handling all the tricky curves of the road. You have a few choices:

> **You can yell and scream at them to settle down.** (Has that ever worked?)

> **You can try to ignore them and press on.** (Ignoring the problem doesn't make it go away.)

> **You can kick them off the bus.** (But that doesn't make them go away.)

I would recommend another choice. Bolstered by your black sheep values, invite your inner critic to the front of the bus and ask two important questions:

> **What do you want to say to me?** By giving your inner critic a voice, you take away their power. Rather than fuel their fire by ignoring them, let them speak. Look for the truth within the hateful talk. Are they saying something that can help you? Are they saying something about the things that matter most to you? If so, address it with your core values in mind. If not, let it go.

What happened to you that makes you think that it's okay to speak to me like this? Try to get to the root of the hurt. Understanding where the negative self-talk is coming from will help you know how to deal with it. Treat your inner critic like a young child. Show them compassion and respect. This will defuse the situation.

After you have this conversation with your inner critic, thank them for their input and tell them to go back and sit in their seat. While they can have a seat on the bus, they are never allowed to touch the steering wheel. Only you take the wheel... and maybe Jesus.

Because Jim Trick was able to figure this out, he lost all the weight again and now maintains a healthy, purposeful lifestyle driven by his core values. Being led by your core values means living with deliberate intention, looking to your black sheep first and showing them to others in every interaction. Your black sheep are designed to be illuminated! That's why I have the black sheep logo tattooed on my right forearm as a constant reminder that black sheep values should be seen first.

How are you going to remind yourself to lead with yours? Are you willing to tattoo a black sheep on your body? If you want to go all-in like I did, I will be happy to provide the artwork to you as long as you send a picture so we can celebrate your commitment. Or you could wear a bracelet of some sort, or do a morning ritual that brings your black sheep to the forefront. Or something else.

Finding and engaging your black sheep is the key to better decisions, a better life and a better world.

Whatever you need to do to remind yourself of your commitment to you, do it.

In bringing your black sheep to the fore, you allow your authentic self to be seen. There is nothing more powerful you can do in your life. You will begin to attract other magnetic people like you. You will notice your impact multiplying. You will start to build a new community around you that will empower you to move toward living your purpose. By speaking your black sheep into existence, you become an original.

Architects can create unique structures by infusing their black sheep into the design process. Photographers can distinguish themselves by capturing their core values along with their subjects in every image. Lawyers can increase the probability of winning by channeling their black sheep to truly connect with the jury. Teachers can inspire better learning by employing their black sheep to develop deeper relationships with their students. Nurses can positively impact the healing process by embodying their black sheep in every patient's room. Congress can fulfill their promises by using their black sheep to honor the will of the people. Financial advisers can generate greater returns for their clients by filtering their decisions through their black sheep to avoid unnecessary risk... This list could go on for another two hundred pages.

If you haven't figured it out by now, your black sheep will lead you to it: You are an extraordinary, awe-inspiring part of this world. Your contribution is uniquely yours. And this world desperately needs it.

Acknowledgments

IN DESCRIBING the type of people he liked to be around, author Mike Yaconelli wrote this in his book *Messy Spirituality*: "I like people who openly admit their 'notoriousness'—people who unabashedly confess they are hopelessly flawed and hopelessly forgiven... whose discipleship is blatantly real and carelessly passionate, characterized by a brazen godliness."

I have lived my life aspiring to be that kind of person. To be a spiritual troublemaker that defies a simple definition. This book is an extension of that desire. It wouldn't have been possible without the belief in that calling for my life by so many.

My wife, Emily, and boys, Theo and Brady—our story is an F'd up fairy tale... but it's ours. The sacrifices you have all made for me have been the greatest gift I've ever received. I love you all. Mom and Dad—I know the path I chose for my life has caused many sleepless nights. Thank you for believing in me even when I didn't believe in myself. Todd, Karrie, Kadence and Avery—your love is the 1,500-mile bridge between us. Mom and Dad Schorr—your faith and love have been a rock for us all. Thank you. Lisa,

Steve, Dylan and Sam—you've walked with us through the valley. I love you for it.

I have been blessed with so many friends that are truly "family" and continue to support my dreams. Pam, JT and Shay, Trick, Jim, Alan and Teresa, PW, Marty and Candy, Bartel, Dave and Jessy, Sherry, Jen, Lee, KT, Melissa, Michael, Karen, Val, Kelly, Rich and countless others that could fill a dozen pages.

The incredible Speak & Spill Mastermind community from the hearts of Scott and Alison Stratten. It has opened the door to decades' worth of incredible insights by some of the best to ever walk onstage. LGO, Ron, Brett, Mitch, Jeffrey, Tom and Tamsen, Neen, Phil M, Alan, Kate, Michael and Amy, Phil G, Alison, Shannon and the five hundred others who raise the bar with every talk... thank you.

Finally, the magical crew of Page Two. Jesse, your belief in this project from our very first conversation gave me the courage to push forward. Kendra, I loved every second of working together. Your quiet confidence was exactly what I needed. Trena, Annemarie, Tilman, Peter, Lorraine, Gabi, Deanna, Mary, Chris and everyone else... you are amazing. Now let's change the world!

About the Author

BRANT MENSWAR is one of the country's "Top 10 Motivational Speakers," a critically acclaimed author, an award-winning musician, a podcast host and the CEO and founder of Rock Star Impact, a boutique agency that teaches people and organizations how to cultivate values-based leadership. His work as a partner with the innovative consulting firm Banding People Together has changed what's possible for industry-leading organizations like Netflix, Verizon, SunTrust, Microsoft, ESPN, Hilton, Sony Pictures, St. Jude Children's Research Hospital and dozens more.

Passionate, engaging and transformational, Brant encourages audiences to move forward with deliberate intention. His interactive and entertaining technique of defining what matters most compels audiences to dive deeper into their lives, identify their core values and give them the airplay needed to become life-changing anthems that change what's possible.

If you are interested in having Brant speak at your event, please visit www.brantmenswar.com.

About Cannonball Kids' cancer (CKc) Foundation

PART OF MY journey with activating my black sheep and being deliberate with my intention has been supporting the amazing work of Cannonball Kids' cancer (CKc) Foundation. A portion of the proceeds from this book goes to support its efforts to provide options to those who have been told they have run out of options. Below you will find some information on what the organization does to bring hope to families battling cancer.

Childhood cancer treatments have gone largely without progressive developments for over twenty years; and, for some forms of childhood cancers, the survival rate is still 0 percent. CKc Foundation is transforming this reality by funding innovative, first-of-its-kind research and educating the public on the realities of childhood cancer, both the rate of survivorship for various cancers and the impact of childhood cancer treatments on survivors. Their rigorous, relationship-based, invite-only grants process ensures that 92 percent of CKc-funded trials are first-of-their-kind in the United States. To date, CKc has awarded $2.4 million, funding twenty-four research grants—which have led to 585 options for treatment for children in twenty-five states, DC, Canada, Scotland and Switzerland.

To learn more about how you can join the fight and become an option for a child in need, please visit:

www.cannonballkidscancer.org.